Celebrating American Holidays

CHRISTMAS

Jill Foran and Jordan McGill

AV² provides enriched content that supplements and complements this book. Weigl's AV² books strive to create inspired learning and engage young minds in a total learning experience.

Your AV² Media Enhanced books come alive with...

Audio
Listen to sections of the book read aloud.

Key Words
Study vocabulary, and complete a matching word activity.

Go to **www.av2books.com**, and enter this book's unique code.

Video
Watch informative video clips.

Quizzes
Test your knowledge.

BOOK CODE

U 8 7 1 2 7 4

Embedded Weblinks
Gain additional information for research.

Slide Show
View images and captions, and prepare a presentation.

AV² by Weigl brings you media enhanced books that support active learning.

Try This!
Complete activities and hands-on experiments.

... and much, much more!

Published by Weigl Publishers Inc.
350 5th Avenue, 59th Floor
New York, NY 10118
Website: www.weigl.com

Library of Congress Cataloging-in-Publication Data

Christmas / edited by Jordan McGill.
    p. cm. -- (Celebrating American holidays: Arts & crafts)
  ISBN 978-1-61690-679-5 (hardcover : alk. paper) -- ISBN 978-1-61690-685-6 (softcover : alk. paper)
  1. Christmas--Juvenile literature. I. McGill, Jordan.
  GT4985.5.C475 2012
  394.2663--dc22
                                2011002422

Printed in the United States of America in North Mankato, Minnesota
1 2 3 4 5 6 7 8 9 0 15 14 13 12 11

062011
WEP290411

Project Coordinator Jordan McGill   **Art Director** Terry Paulhus

Every reasonable effort has been made to trace ownership and to obtain permission to reprint copyright material. The publishers would be pleased to have any errors or omissions brought to their attention so that they may be corrected in subsequent printings.

Weigl acknowledges Getty Images as its primary image supplier for this title. Craft photos by Madison Helton.

CONTENTS

AV² Book Code 2

What is Christmas? 4

History of Christmas 6

The Child of Christmas 8

Celebrating Today 10

Christmas Tree 12

Christmas Cards 14

Santa Claus 16

Songs of Joy 18

Christmas Food 20

What Have You Learned? 22

Glossary/Index 23

Log on to www.av2books.com 24

10

13

16

21

3

What is Christmas?

Christmas is one of the most popular holidays in the United States. It is also an important religious celebration. Americans are filled with feelings of good will during the Christmas season. They honor many Christmas **customs**. People all across the country decorate their homes with lights and ornaments. They exchange gifts with friends and loved ones. Families share Christmas feasts.

The Christmas season begins in early December. This is when people start to put up their decorations and shop for presents. **Carolers** sing Christmas songs throughout the season. Christmas Day is always celebrated on December 25. The Christmas season usually ends in early January.

History of Christmas

Christmas celebrates the birth of Jesus Christ. **Christians** believe that Jesus was the son of God. In AD 336, the leaders of the Roman Catholic Church made an important decision. They decided that Jesus' birthday would always be celebrated on December 25. This date was chosen because December was already a festive time of year. For many years, the Romans had held a festival called Saturnalia in December.

During Saturnalia, the Romans lit candles as a symbol of Saturn's light. They would place the candles on trees in honor of Saturn. Christians began following the **tradition**. Christians placed a candle on a tree as a **symbol** of the star that led people to the place where Jesus was born.

As time passed, people all over Europe began to celebrate Christmas. They mixed Christian customs with customs from other winter festivals. When European **settlers** moved to the United States, they continued to celebrate their Christmas traditions.

Light a Candle

Follow these instructions to make a candle for your Christmas tree.

What You Need

- paper towel or toilet paper tube
- white glue
- paint
- white paper
- scissors
- crayons or markers

7 Easy Steps to Complete Your Candle

1 Stand the tube up. Apply white glue to the top of the tube so that it runs down over the tube. It should look like a dripping candle. Then, cut a circular piece of paper, and cover the top of the roll with it.

2 Let the glue dry.

3 Paint the tube any color you like.

4 Cut a piece of paper into the shape of a flame.

5 Using crayons or markers, color the paper so that it looks like a flame.

6 Stand the paper tube up, and glue the paper flame to the top of it.

7 Have an adult help you put it at the top of your Christmas tree.

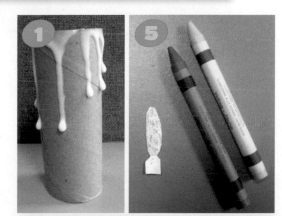

The Child of Christmas

The story of Jesus' birth is told in the Bible. It begins with a woman named Mary, who lived in a city called Nazareth. One night, an angel visited Mary and told her that she was chosen to be the mother of God's son.

Shortly after the angel's visit, Mary married a man named Joseph. As the time for Jesus' birth drew near, Joseph took Mary to the town of Bethlehem. When they arrived in the city, all of the inns were full. An innkeeper let Mary and Joseph stay in his stable. That night, Mary gave birth to Jesus in the stable. Three shepherds and three wise men came to visit him.

Make a Diorama

A diorama is a model. Follow the instructions below to make a model of the night Jesus was born.

What You Need

- modeling clay
- small box
- dried grass
- black and yellow construction paper
- paints or markers
- glue

7 Easy Steps to Complete Your Diorama

1 Cut off the flaps of the box. Lay the box on its side with the opening facing you.

2 Make a background for your scene. Use glue to cover the walls and ceiling of the box with black construction paper. This is the sky. Cover the box's floor with yellow construction paper.

3 Cut an eight-pointed star from the paper. Color it gold or yellow. Glue it high up on the middle of the box.

4 Place grass around the inside of the box to create the manger.

5 Use modeling clay to make the figures of Joseph, Mary, the baby Jesus, and three wise men. You can use toothpicks to make them stand up. Form a small base out of modeling clay for each figure, and stick a toothpick in it. Place the clay figure on the toothpick. You can also make farm animals, including a sheep, a donkey, or a camel.

6 Color the clay figures and scenery to add detail.

7 Once you have placed all the characters and scenery, use glue to secure them to the box.

Celebrating Today

Today, Christmas is a time for visiting loved ones. It is also a time to enjoy music, decorations, and tasty treats. Families and friends buy presents for each other at Christmas. The gifts are wrapped in **festive** paper and placed under the Christmas tree. Gifts remain untouched under the tree until they are opened on Christmas Eve or Christmas Day.

Many Christian families attend church services at Christmas. Special midnight **masses** are held on Christmas Eve. These masses honor the Christian belief that Jesus was born close to midnight.

Wrap a Present

Christmas wrapping paper can be shiny, sparkly, or have Christmas scenes on it. This activity will help you make wrapping paper for your gifts.

What You Need

- large paper
- paint
- sponges
- paper
- scissors
- plastic or paper plates

5 Easy Steps to Complete Your Christmas Wrapping Paper

1. Cut the sponges into Christmas shapes, such as a Christmas tree, star, or candy cane.

2. Place the paper in front of you.

3. Put the paint on the paper plate. You can have several colors on the plate at the same time.

4. Dip the different sponges into the paint. Press the sponge onto the paper. Repeat this step until you are satisfied with how the paper looks.

5. Let the paper dry. Now you are ready to wrap a present with your wrapping paper.

Christmas Tree

The Christmas tree is a popular symbol of Christmas. The custom of decorating Christmas trees began in the early 1600s. One Christmas night, a German man named Martin Luther noticed how lovely the **evergreens** looked in the starlight. He cut down a small tree, took it home, and decorated it with candles.

Soon, Christmas trees were popular all over Germany. German settlers brought the custom to the United States in the 1700s. Today, every state in the country grows trees for Christmas. These trees are grown on special farms.

Hang an Ornament

People often put ornaments on their tree for decoration. Make your own ornament using these instructions.

What You Need

- Styrofoam (TM) ball
- sequins or beads
- glue
- gold string
- black marker
- scissors

4 Easy Steps to Complete Your Ornament

1. Lightly draw a pattern onto the Styrofoam ball.

2. Cut a loop of gold string. Make sure the loop is long enough to go around the branch of a Christmas tree. Use a dab of glue to hold the ends of the loop together. Glue the entire loop to the top of the Styrofoam ball.

3. Glue the sequins or beads onto the ball in the pattern you drew. Let the glue dry.

4. Hang the ornament on your Christmas tree, or give it to a friend as a gift.

Christmas Cards

Sending greeting cards is a Christmas custom. The cards often use words such as "Merry Christmas," "Happy Holidays," or "Season's Greetings." Sending Christmas cards has been popular in the United States since the late 1800s.

Today, people send Christmas cards to their friends, family, and relatives all over the world. Many people who are not Christian give or receive Christmas cards during the holiday.

Send a Christmas Greeting

Many people like to receive homemade Christmas cards. You can make your own cards by following these instructions.

What You Need

- piece of thick white paper
- red glitter paint
- scissors
- red ribbon

7 Easy Steps to Complete Your Card

1 Draw a large candy cane shape on the paper. Then, cut it out.

2 Draw lines up and around the candy cane.

3 Fill in every second section with red glitter paint. Be sure to leave one white section between each pair of red sections.

4 Cut out a small card from the remaining white paper. Write a Christmas message on the inside of your card.

5 Tie a bow with the red ribbon.

6 Glue the ribbon to the top bend of the candy cane. Then, glue the cane and bow to the front of the card. Seal with tape.

7 Present your candy cane card to a friend or relative.

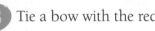

15

Santa Claus

Children all over the United States eagerly await a visit from Santa Claus on Christmas Eve. Santa Claus is believed to visit homes long after everyone goes to sleep. He flies through the sky in a sleigh that is pulled by eight reindeer.

Santa Claus stops at every house, leaving gifts for children who have been good. He places them under the Christmas tree or in Christmas stockings.

Wear a Santa Hat

Santa Claus wears a special red hat to keep his head warm. This activity will let you make a Santa hat of your own.

What You Need

- large sheet of red construction paper
- cotton balls
- glue

4 Easy Steps to Complete Your Santa Hat

1 Draw a half circle on the red construction paper. Take up as much of the sheet as possible. Then, cut the half circle out.

2 Take both ends of the half circle and roll them together so that the cutout becomes a cone. Glue the seam together, and let the glue dry.

3 Glue cotton balls along the bottom of the cone. Glue one cotton ball on the pointy tip of the cone. Let the glue dry.

4 Now you can wear a Santa hat to a holiday celebration.

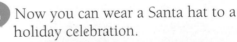

Songs of Joy

During the Christmas season, Christmas music can be heard almost everywhere. These special songs help people enjoy the holiday season.

Christmas songs of praise and joy are called carols. Most carols describe the events of Jesus' birth. Some carols have been sung for hundreds of years.

O Little Town of Bethlehem

O little town of Bethlehem
How still we see thee lie
Above thy deep and dreamless sleep
The silent stars go by
Yet in thy dark streets shineth
The everlasting Light
The hopes and fears of all the years
Are met in thee tonight

For Christ is born of Mary
And gathered all above
While mortals sleep, the angels keep
Their watch of wondering love
O morning stars together
Proclaim the holy birth
And praises sing to God the King
And Peace to men on earth

How silently, how silently
The wondrous gift is given!
So God imparts to human hearts
The blessings of His heaven.
No ear may his His coming,
But in this world of sin,
Where meek souls will receive him still,
The dear Christ enters in.

O holy Child of Bethlehem
Descend to us, we pray
Cast out our sin and enter in
Be born to us today
We hear the Christmas angels
The great glad tidings tell
O come to us, abide with us
Our Lord Emmanuel

Write a Christmas Carol

Write your own Christmas song lyrics using the chart below and the words at the bottom of the page. How many Christmas words can you use in your Christmas song?

1 Start brainstorming ideas. What do you want your song to be about? Choose an event, idea, person, or feeling you would like to write about.

2 Many songs have a chorus. The chorus is the main idea of the song. It connects the verses and is repeated several times. Write a chorus for your song.

3 Write the verses. Songs usually have three to four verses. Each one will be different, but all should relate to the chorus. The final verse ends the song.

4 Once you have written your song, read over the lyrics again. Are there any changes you could make to improve the song? Work on the words until you are happy with them.

Christmas Words

Christmas	Tree	Decorate	Ornament	Light	Roman	Festive
Santa	Cookies	Candle	Custom	Candy Cane	Song	Joy
Card	Rudolph	Gift	Carol	Stocking	Wrap	Nativity
Jesus	Saturnalia	Feast				

Christmas Food

Everyone looks forward to the delicious foods served during Christmas time. Many people bake special treats for their friends and neighbors. Some of the best Christmas treats include fruitcakes, **mince pies**, and gingerbread cookies. Children often build gingerbread houses with the cookies. These houses can be decorated with frosting, jellybeans, gummy candies, and candy canes.

Most families gather for a huge meal on Christmas Day or Christmas Eve. Traditional Christmas feasts usually include roasted turkey with stuffing, cranberry sauce, mashed potatoes, and rich desserts.

Bake Gingerbread Cookies

Gingerbread cookies are a great Christmas treat!

What You Need

- 2 teaspoons ground ginger
- 3 cups flour
- 2/3 cup shortening
- 1/2 cups brown sugar
- 1 teaspoon cinnamon
- 1/4 teaspoon ground cloves
- 3/4 cup molasses
- 1 large egg
- Pinch of salt
- 1/2 teaspoon of baking powder
- 1 teaspoon of baking soda
- frosting
- candy decorations

9 Easy Steps to Bake Your Cookies

1. Mix the shortening, brown sugar, cinnamon, cloves, ginger, and salt in a large bowl.

2. Crack the egg into the bowl, and blend the ingredients together. Then, add the molasses, and mix again.

3. In a separate bowl, blend the flour, baking powder, and baking soda. Add the dry ingredients to the other bowl. Mix all of the ingredients together to make dough.

4. Once everything is completely mixed, place the bowl in the fridge for at least one hour.

5. Heat the oven to 375 degrees Fahrenheit. Roll the dough into a large ball, and then flatten it with a rolling pin.

6. Cut out gingerbread man shapes.

7. Place the cookies in the oven, and bake for 10 minutes.

8. Remove the cookies from the oven, and let them cool down.

9. Decorate your cookies with frosting and candy. Then, add the gingerbread men to a gingerbread house or share them with family and friends.

What Have You Learned?

1 When does the Christmas season begin?

2 What does Christmas traditionally celebrate?

3 Who decided what day the birth of Jesus Christ would fall on?

4 What Roman holiday influenced Christmas traditions?

5 On what day are Christmas gifts opened?

6 Where did the idea of a Christmas tree originate?

7 Who visits houses late on Christmas Eve?

Answers
1. Early December 2. Christmas celebrates the birth of Jesus 3. The Roman Catholic Church 4. Saturnalia 5. Christmas Eve or Christmas Day 6. Germany 7. Santa Claus

Glossary

carolers: people who sing Christmas carols

Christians: people who believe that Jesus was the son of God

customs: ways of acting that have become habit

evergreens: trees that stay green throughout the year

festive: joyous; merry

masses: a type of church service

mince pies: special holiday pies filled with fruit, nuts, raisins, and sometimes meat

settlers: people who moved to a new country to live

symbol: something that represents something else

tradition: a custom or way of doing something

Index

carols 5, 18

Christian 6, 10, 14

church 6

Jesus 6, 8, 9, 10, 18, 22

Romans 6, 22

Saturnalia 6

23

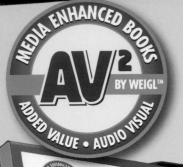

Log on to www.av2books.com

AV² by Weigl brings you media enhanced books that support active learning. Go to www.av2books.com, and enter the special code found on page 2 of this book. You will gain access to enriched and enhanced content that supplements and complements this book. Content includes video, audio, web links, quizzes, a slide show, and activities.

Audio
Listen to sections of the book read aloud.

Video
Watch informative video clips.

Embedded Weblinks
Gain additional information for research.

Try This!
Complete activities and hands-on experiments.

WHAT'S ONLINE?

Try This!	Embedded Weblinks	Video	EXTRA FEATURES
Try more fun activities.	Find out more about the history of Christmas.	Watch a video about Christmas.	**Audio** Listen to sections of the book read aloud.
Write a biography about an important person.	Find out more about an important holiday symbol.	Check out another video about Christmas.	**Key Words** Study vocabulary, and complete a matching word activity.
Make another recipe.	Read more information about Christmas.		**Slide Show** View images and captions and prepare a presentatio
Play an interactive activity.	Find out about a similar celebration.		**Quizzes** Test your knowledge.

AV² was built to bridge the gap between print and digital. We encourage you to tell us what you like and what you want to see in the future.

Sign up to be an AV² Ambassador at www.av2books.com/ambassador.